5 Paragraph Business Plan

The Action Oriented Business Management Tool for Leaders

5

Tips, tricks, and tutorials found at 5Paragraph.com

Complete a call with one of our advisors and receive a free workbook to get you started.

We offer in-person advising and instruction to include corporate retreats, event workshops, and keynotes by U.S. military veterans who are adding VALUE to the world.

Index

Intent

The "5 paragraph Business Plan" is a simple military-style business planning and management tool. The tool was built using the 5-paragraph operations order; developed by the U. S. Military and the reference book "The Nuts and Bolts of Great Business Plans"; developed by IVMF: Institute of Veterans Military and Families as part of the EBV: Entrepreneurship Bootcamp for Veterans curriculum. Each method for planning and executing a mission, whether it be military or business, has the same desired effect in mind; to commit action towards a valuable objective. Two proven planning methods, tested on the battlefield and in the boardroom, combined into a single action-oriented business management tool: the **5 Paragraph Business Plan.** This guidebook walks through the "5 Paragraph Business Plan" and the detailed subparagraphs that make up the plan. Read through this guidebook and listen through the tutorials at 5Paragraph.com to help construct your overall plan.

Every reader is both a creator and executor of the plan. The "5 Paragraph Business Plan" is for entrepreneurs and intrepreneurial business leaders who desire a simpler and more effective way to strategize and execute missions in the modern business world. This model of planning is based on the United States military operations order, typically used by the U.S. Army and U.S. Marine Corps. Military planning methods have been honed over the past 240 years. They rely on ancient knowledge of human nature, a sense of cultural understanding and the ability to study the enemy's use of tactics, techniques, and procedures. For years, business leaders have read "The Art of War". Sun Tzu, and various military officers, illustrate the art of tactical decision making in a variety of circumstances using a variety of disciplines. Business concepts and strategy in war are similar – but here's where the analogy is broken.

In war, the enemy is a person or a group, not so in business. The enemy is not a person or another company. **The enemy is the NEED**, the problem/opportunity that must be addressed with the VALUE of goods, products and/or, services. The "5 Paragraph Business Plan" provides you with a method for locating and destroying that NEED. It guides you through mapping out the size and activity in an industry and enables the creator and executor of the plan to precisely target markets and deliver VALUE. This concept of the enemy/NEED is found throughout the text and templates. It is important to cultivate a warrior mentality toward destroying the NEED. It is the purpose of a company to destroy the problems faced by a population of people in demand. They have a NEED for the VALUE your company provides. Attack that NEED with the same ferocity that you would attack an enemy. From now on the NEED is your enemy - crush it.

The "5 Paragraph Business Plan" keeps the whole organization on the same page. A combination of military combat arms strategy, small unit leadership tactics, and operational planning structures; coupled with business knowledge and experience in company creation, execution, and sustainable operations. Proven business practices combined with 240 years of warfighting, developed into one tool, the "5 Paragraph Business Plan".

Acknowledgments

To the men and women who are serving or have ever served this nation with honor and selfless sacrifice, thank you for your steadfast devotion to our way of life and liberty.

You are the best of us.

The creators of the "5 Paragraph Business Plan" owe a huge debt of gratitude for the education and experience provided by our U.S. military. The armed forces do an outstanding job of taking young men and women from fledgling pupils to battle ready warriors. Those with a burning desire to serve will find themselves among the world's very best.

The military and society play a symbiotic role in America. An all-volunteer force of men and women, all from wildly different backgrounds and upbringings, unite for the common purpose of national defense. For that time in service, the team comes first. The mission takes precedence. The individual is an afterthought. Everyone is instructed in the basics of how to perform the duties pertaining to their military occupational specialty. Promotion is based on proficiency in the service member's given specialty, their instructor abilities, and ability to lead. A service member is provided with opportunities to learn advanced techniques within their specialty, potentially becoming instructors and instructor trainers. They may attend leadership schools pertaining to advanced levels of delegation and supervision. The accumulative school accreditations and situationally dependent decision-making experience adds up to a well-rounded warrior. Combine that with experience planning and conducting field operations, and potentially combat experience, you get a high output asset that can uplift the whole organization; IF empowered. After leaving the military, many veterans choose to head back to their home of record. They bring those skills knowledge and experience along with them. This book is an example of that.

Thank you for taking the time to read and use this text for your own gain. It is our sincere hope that you use all the tools we provide at 5Paragraph.com to build your own organization and achieve success in whatever endeavor you choose to take on. Add VALUE to the world and continue to work with a purpose. We only ask that you share your success story with others by telling them about 5Paragraph.com and all that we have to offer. Together we can make sense of the chaos and get to work turning your vision into reality.

Thank you for your time and efforts. Stay the course. Take care and be well.

INVICTUS

-by William Ernest Henley

Out of the night that covers me,
Black as the pit from pole to pole,
I thank whatever gods may be
For my unconquerable soul.

In the fell clutch of circumstance
I have not winced nor cried aloud.
Under the bludgeonings of chance
My head is bloody, but unbowed.

Beyond this place of wrath and tears
Looms but the Horror of the shade,
And yet the menace of the years
Finds and shall find me unafraid.

It matters not how strait the gate,
How charged with punishments the scroll,
I am the master of my fate,
I am the captain of my soul.

U.S. Military 5 PARAGRAPH ORDER || O-SMEAC

Orientation - To familiarize the operations team with their surroundings prior to issuing the order. In reference to map: Current location, friendly locations, enemy activity, civilian activity, terrain and weather considerations, environmental atmospherics: sunrise, sunset, twilight, night time visibility, estimated time of operation; area of operation, key locations.

I. **Situation**
    A. Enemy Forces
        Enemy Situation (SALUTE) Size, Activity, Location, Unit, Time (observed), Equipment
        Enemy's Capabilities/Limitations (DRAW-D) Defend, Reinforce, Attack, Withdraw, Delay
        Enemy's Most Probable Course of Action (EMPCOA)
    B. Friendly Forces
        Higher Command's Mission & Intent
        Adjacent Units
            North/ South/ East/ West
            Same Echelon
        Supporting
    C. Attachments/Detachments
II. **Mission**
    Who, What, Where, When, and (most importantly) Why?
III. **Execution**
    A. Commander's Intent
        Center of Gravity
        Critical Vulnerability
        Exploitation Plan
        Desired End State
    B. Concept of the Operation
        Scheme of Maneuver
        Fire Support Plan
    C. Tasks
    D. Coordinating Instructions
IV. **Administration/ Logistics || Sustainment**
    A. Administration - "Bad Guys & Bandages": EPW & CASEVAC Plans
    B. Logistics - "Beans, Bullets, & Batteries": Chow, Ammo, Supply, Comms, Pyro, etc.
V. **Command/ Signal || Command & Control**
    A. Location of Key Leaders
    B. Succession of Command

Preparation – Industry/ Market Analysis

METT-TSL: Mission, Enemy, Team & Support, Terrain & weather - Time available, Space Available, Logistics

---

This is your starting template. As you read the "5 Paragraph Business Plan" guidebook look for the METT-TSL call out boxes, like the one above. Use the METT-TSL template to find the basic elements for your plan. Fill in the template as best you can and know that you can come back to complete parts over time as you gather information. You will be able to fill in the gaps while reading through the text. Keep an open mind and don't be afraid to make changes to the template. METT-TSL provides a basic overall structure to your plan. Each element is crucial for company success in the long term. It is important to start with this shortened METT-TSL template prior to building out an entire business plan.

Mission
Who, What, Where, When, and Why
- The company and concept.
- The product and or service.
- Entry and growth strategy.

Enemy – the problem, the *NEED or demand* (*problem you will solve*).
Summarize the industry in which the proposed business will operate.

Industry/ Market
- Discuss briefly industry size (in Dollars) and annual growth rate (%).
- Discuss the structure of the industry at present.

SALUTE: Size, Activity, Location, Uniform, Time, Equipment

Center of Gravity, Critical Vulnerability, Exploitation Plan
- Market segmentation and target market.
- Estimated market share and sales figures.

Enemy's Most Deadly Course of Action
- Discuss assumptions implicit in the plan.
- Identify and discuss any major problems and other risks.
- Address assumptions/ potential problems/ risks critical to the success of the venture.

Team & Support

Size of the Team; 4, 12, 42.

Capabilities, Features, Unfair Advantage
- Organization.
- Key management and personnel.
- Management compensation and ownership.
- Other current investors.
- Employment and other agreements, stock options and, bonus plans.
- Board of directors or board of advisors.
- Other shareholders, rights and, restrictions.
- Supporting professional advisors and services.

Terrain & Weather

General Location; Environmental Conditions, Seasonal Dependents, Geography.

Time

Schedule until market - 3-6-9-month projection; 3-5-year growth strategy.
- Current trends [3-6 months].
- Long term trends [2-5 years].
- Provide standard financial ratios for the industry.

Space

Development Iterations – [Seen Obstacles to Success].

Logistics

Barriers to Entry; Capital, Equipment, Transportation, Technology...etc.

Paragraph 1: Situation – Market research findings

This section of the "5 Paragraph Business Plan" is for you the business plan creator to *show your work* as to how you've drawn your market conclusions. Thoroughly check all data and alternative sources of market data prior to constructing a full plan.

You must fully explain your market research – how many people responded to surveys, example quotes, how many conversations you had with customers, the results from other data collection, etc. Everything you've done in part to create the image of the market you are presenting to investors, proving that you truly understand your customers.

You, the business creator, must provide evidence of what you did and what results came out of it. The reader of your final plan must be convinced that your product or service provides a solution to your customer's problem (the NEED you are fulfilling) and customers will want the solution you are presenting them; as well as proof that potential customers exist - so many customers in fact that there is a substantial market inside of a growing industry; and finally, you need to show how you will generate earnings in a competitive landscape. A simple way of demonstrating true understanding of the market is by showing sound sales projections. Market research determines the plan's structure and operations within. Sales projections include the equity capital and debt needed for manufacturing operations, marketing and advertising. The results paint the future image of your business in the long term.

Most entrepreneurs do not present adequate market research and competitive analyses to prove their sales estimates are achievable.

Market research starts at the public library. All major data collection done by large market research firms first passed through libraries and depositories. Catalogues of information and eager librarians await at your public library. Call ahead to see what information they require to get a card. Typically, it's only a driver's license and proof of residence and you have access to even more information than what's provided on the web.

Research industry publications, trade articles and magazines, trade associations and journals to gain a clear perspective on the industry you are competing in. Identify customer segments and target markets. Compile all the information into a concise way by using the "5 Paragraph Business Plan". All this information plugs into the 'enemy' portion of the METT-TSL template that was provided earlier.

This section of the '5 Paragraph Business Plan' is the most difficult to prepare and is arguably the most important. The rest of the plan depends on the market research and analysis presented here. Be advised: prepare this section with great attention to detail. Other parts of the plan rely heavily on the market analysis collected and presented in this section of the plan.

Situation

A. Industry: **Market Research & Analysis**
Define the problem that your company will address.

Defining the problem that your company will address. The problem / opportunity and the reason for starting your business. The enemy is the problem your target customer has. Business is derived from the opportunity to capitalize on delivering a solution for that NEED. Think of the industry as a large area of operation. The industry is broken down into smaller markets. A market must be monopolized to grow outside of that market and gain greater traction throughout the industry.

---

* METT-TSL: **Enemy** - identify the size and scope of the problem/opportunity

---

S.A.L.U.T.E.

Size -	Size of the industry - size of the market you wish to attack.
Activity -	Recent activity within the market - key overall trends.
Location -	Where your customer lives - where they shop and purchase your value.
Unit -	Develop your ideal customer - build an avatar to sell to.
Time -	When customers typically purchase - when they are looking for your value.
Equipment -	Equipment you need to deliver / equipment the customer needs to purchase.

1. Industry's Composition, Disposition, Strength
   Summarize the industry in which the proposed business will operate.
   - Market segmentation and target market.
   - Estimated market share and sales figures.
   - Buyer demographics and buyer behavior.
   - Definition of your relevant market and customer overview.
   - Size of the market and the overall trends in activity.
   - Location where business is conducted [online/brick & mortar].
   - Uniform; avatar of your ideal consumer: age, gender, marital status, level of education, household income.

---

* METT-TSL: **Terrain & weather**: How will the *elements* affect the business?

---

2. Market's Capabilities & Limitations
   - Discuss briefly industry size (in Dollars) and annual growth rate (%).
   - Discuss the structure of the industry at present.
   - Highlight key trends in the industry at present.
   - **highlight Key trends in the industry.**
   - Fluctuations in the market in the past 3-5 years.
     - Why this is good, bad or, ugly.

3. Market's Most Likely Course of Action: **Given the current solution being provided, the 'most likely course of action' is a prediction for how the market will react based upon** *previous results.*
   - Current trends [3-6 months].
   - Long term trends [2-5 years].
   - Provide standard financial ratios for the industry.

4. Market's Most Probable Course of Action: **This is where you provide an assumption for the probable course of action the market will take to alleviate the problem. This is how other companies may be attempting to tackle the problem right now. The 'most probable course of action' is a prediction for how the market will react based upon the current solution being offered.**
   - Where the market is going based upon intelligence analysis.
   - Ongoing market evaluation.
   - Determine the key success factors for the industry and draw conclusions.

5. Market's Most Dangerous Course of Action: **This is what will happen if the current problem persists and is able to grow out of control without any intervention. The 'most deadly course of action' is the absolute worst case scenario for the market if** no one **presents a solution.**

Critical Risks, Problems & Assumptions

Take the time to walk through market scenarios involving your value offering, whether that's a product or service. Talk about the bad up front. Demonstrate a clear understanding of your industry. Highlight the hardest problems facing a business in your target market. Tell everyone how you offer a winning solution by creating an intelligence picture around your business and the product or service you provide. Share your market insights and how they translate into a plan for mitigating failure.
   - Discuss assumptions implicit in the plan and back them up with facts.
   - Identify and discuss any major problems and other risks.
   - Address assumptions/ potential problems/ risks critical to the success of the venture.

---

* ME**TT**-T**S**L: **T**eam & **S**upport: This is where the competition gets 'sized up'. You need to know who the competition is and what they are up to. Often, competitors in the market can be the best of friends. In today's modern startup environment, it's hard to find a "direct competitor." Companies thrive on the ability to diversify and help more consumers. Assisting a competitor in their adjacent mission can pay huge dividends when leveraging a competitor's support in the future. Plus, competition brings more consumers; they want to see what all the hype is about.

Use the following S.A.L.U.T.E. template to conduct a report on your own target market.

SIZE

ACTIVITY

LOCATION

UNIT / UNIFORM

TIME

EQUIPMENT

B. Friendly Forces

6. Higher Command's Mission & Intent
   - List the large competitors that will be disrupted by your activity.
   - List the perceived objectives of key industry players.

7. Adjacent Companies; Competition – Friend or Foe
   - Competition and competitive edges.
     Location –
       o Collaborator's locations.
       o Direct competitor's locations.
       o Goals & objectives; friends and competitors.

8. Supporting Companies
   - Supplier raw materials, goods, items etc.
   - Customer service, virtual assistance, scheduling software, customer relationship management software etc.

C. Attachments/Detachments; these are outsourced staff or contractors' imperative to mission success
   - **Supporting professional advisors and services.**
   - Freelance staff or contractors.
   - Interns earning class credit with pay or otherwise.

Attachments and detachments may also include supporting companies who have bartered their goods or services in exchange for an asset or time associated with supporting their own efforts. This is the result of "goodwill" through relationship building. The majority of *business* involves relationship building and emotional intelligence. When developing a business, it is crucial that the leadership know how to harness the value within their firm. That value may be used as an offering to adjacent elements within a company or offered to outside companies to further grow both organizations. A symbiotic relationship in the truest sense of the phrase.

This is often overlooked by entrepreneurs and business leaders. The products or services your company provides within a team, section, division, or the overall company may be used as an asset to be leveraged for additional support and may alleviate otherwise costly expenses pertaining to overall mission success. Leverage the value that your organization offers in exchange for the value they provide. That value is part of each organization's overall mission. It's why the organization was created and continues to exist.

D. Civil/Terrain Considerations

- Provide a description of the outside civil considerations - foot traffic near your business location; rerouting of a major vehicle traffic route, such as a highway; city plans for urban, commercial, residential development.
- Specific to the location(s) of your organization and associated locations where any member of your team may be working.
- Consider the general atmosphere of where you want to start your business.

  Where are you going to "set up shop"?

  What is the overall population like in your target area? What is their ethnicity, education, income, living standards, schools, public facilities, distance to amenities etc.?

  Does the neighborhood want your business there?

  Does your business model work against the "goodwill" of the people you *aren't* trying to serve?

  How could this affect your business?

  What is the crime rate in the area you wish to operate your business?
  - Highlight additional considerations based on objectives within the operational plans; specific civil/terrain considerations for an event or function that is necessary for overall mission success.
  - Attending trade shows, meetings, events, conventions

Summarize the scope of the work necessary for your business to be a success given these considerations. Emotional intelligence is key when considering how the population, outside of your target market, may react to your entrance into the market place. It is worth your time to consider those individuals who may not see the value in your product and mitigate the outside risk of potential failure.

> * METT-TSL: **T**errain & Weather: Take the time to consider all aspects of the terrain and how the environment may affect your business venture. There may be elements of the business plan that could be affected by weather and unforeseen environmental disasters, which would inhibit your ability to thrive as a company. Prove to your team, and potential shareholders, that you have thought through the risks assumed by all businesses that operate within your industry.

Paragraph 2: Mission Directives & Statement

This portion of the "5 Paragraph Business Plan" focuses on your venture. A venture is defined as, a risky or daring undertaking. Draw upon elements of the situation paragraph to create your mission statement. A strong mission statement demonstrates true understanding of your target market. Prove your business comprehension by outlining the size and scope of the overall problem/opportunity. Share the size of the industry and target market in numbers. Briefly describe the type of business you have; the solution (good, product, service) you provide.

Mission Directives

First, explain what you are doing to provide a solution for the problem/opportunity, in plain terms. Outline the basic elements of your mission.

- Who you are helping - basic customer profile [soccer moms, veterans, elderly etc.]
- What you are doing to help - good, product, service
- Where customers purchase - online, storefront, by phone
- When this is happening - timeline
- Why you are doing this - show us the passion

There are distinct objectives for every mission. The same is true for business. There are distinct objectives that must be accomplished for the mission to be a success. This overarching mission will be the foundation for all other business operations and should include the values and ethics of the overall organization. It is the key to cultivating a long-term business culture. The values and ethics of an organization shine through in the employees who embody the mission of the company. Your mission statement and the mission directives provide long term guidance for how to act in the future. These elements are the bedrock for creating a code of conduct within the company. Think long term when creating the mission statement and mission directives. If applied correctly, this will develop into a flourishing culture.

Given the mission statement and mission directives, construct an outline of the overall, long term, mission. First outline the essence of your entity. Describe what type of business: retail, online, brick & mortar etc. If you are establishing a business, highlight any progress you've made thus far. Second, highlight the nature of your business concept in a clear and concise fashion, and outline the goods, products and/or services you'll provide. Lastly, describe your entry strategy and, in brief detail, provide a clear vision for how you'll grow the venture over the next 3-5 years. You need to think long term. Outline the Company and Concept. Outline the Product and or Service. Outline Entry and Growth Strategy.

* **METT-TSL: Mission** - The final *mission* in your METT-TSL template is a boiled down summary of all the details of the long-term mission statement and directives. This condensed mission summary proves your value and demonstrates your ability to, potentially, make a return on investment, disrupt a market, succeed in the long term. The key is to get people to ask you *HOW* you're going to accomplish the mission.

Developing your Mission

Write out the VALUES of your company or organization.
1)

2)

3)

Write out the characteristics of your ideal company based on these VALUES.
1)

2)

3)

Write out the characteristics of your ideal team member based on these VALUES.
1)

2)

3)

Create your own Mission Statement
Who, What, Where, When, Why [...HOW?]
- The Company and Concept
- The Product and or Service
- Entry and Growth Strategy

EX.

_____ is a _____ company with a focus on_____ and _____ products for a _____ in order to _____.

MISSION:

Paragraph 3: Execution - *HOW you are going to accomplish the mission*

The execution paragraph is the 'meat and potatoes' of your plan. In the situation paragraph, you outlined the size and scope of the problem/opportunity, as you see it, based on the market research that you've conducted. In the situation paragraph, you've shared the intelligence gathered about what other companies are doing to provide a solution to the problem right now, based on your market analysis. With that intelligence, you have constructed a mission statement and long-term mission directives. You have told us that there is a problem in the world that you would like to solve. You've told us what you are intending to do about the problem, now it's time you tell us *HOW* you are going to make that solution a reality. Keep in mind, we are talking about how the overall business will become established and function in the long term. Elements of the execution paragraph will require great amounts of time and energy being devoted to large scale operations. More detailed operational plans will be constructed in the future by drawing upon elements of this large-scale execution paragraph. You will see a great example of this in the section titled 'Using The "5 Paragraph Business Plan" as an Operational Leader", covered later in this guidebook.

The "5 Paragraph Business Plan" is a structured method for planning and executing operations. In the later portions of this guidebook, you'll see how business leaders throughout the various ranks use this planning method for more detailed individual operations. Use the execution paragraph to outline objectives and assign teams to accomplish them. These objectives become the mission statement directives inside of the operational leader's "5 Paragraph Business Plan". Each objective that has been assigned to a team leader must have a plan constructed to attack that segment of the greater market or executive level mission.

Execution – Company *<Culture>* Operational Strategies

Begin by identifying the largest sources of revenue and how much margin is available on each of them. Economics of business is the basic logic of how profits are earned in a business as well as the sales level required to breakeven. The execution paragraph breaks down the largest potential market with the largest margins to gain and the critical vulnerability within the target market. An exploitation plan is developed to capitalize on the market opportunities available in the targeted area of vulnerability. It is important to highlight this. The exploitation plan is an outline of the overall mid-term goals of the company. These mid-term objectives must be accomplished for long-term mission success.

This large-scale "5 Paragraph Business Plan" concept of operations and overall scheme of how the organization will maneuver is a general outline for the whole business. Smaller, more detailed, "5 Paragraph Business Plans" are created by subordinate team leaders within the larger entity, in order to complete short-term objectives such as sales. Every team leader in your business needs a copy of this book to work off. This is how general officers in the United States military coordinate ongoing operations with small unit leaders in the field. It has been refined over 240 years, it works. Build your culture from the mission statement and directives.

Empower your leaders by providing them with a structured outline for doing business. Task leaders with objectives, enable them to take initiative, in the best interests of the organization.

Execution

Commander's Intent - This is YOUR intent. Tell everyone how you want others to perceive your organization and the team you are employing. The intentions of your organization rest upon the values of your organization. The purpose of accomplishing the overall mission in a professional manner. Based on the **leadership's goals and company's mission statement & directives** the commander's intent is always to win, but to what purpose, under what guidelines of conduct. It is in this small section of the plan that you convey the purpose for executing the mission you outlined earlier. The intent at the lowest level coincides with the overall mission. Build your culture through empowerment.

A. Commander's Intent: at the discretion of the organizational leadership
1. Center of Gravity; biggest pot of gold in the industry or broader overall market.
   - Provide revenue drivers and profit margins (contribution margins).
     - o Driving demand for - Customer service, high quality, low wait time.
   - Outline the overall market landscape and the largest opportunity.
   - Where is the market *pulling* by demanding a solution?
   - What is the largest earning potential in the market?
   - Companies with the most efficient system of delivery earn.
2. Critical Vulnerability; low hanging fruit.
   - Market entry point.
   - Smaller market; easier to monopolize.
   - Fixed and variable costs.
   - Operating leverage and its implications.
   - Low startup costs.

The **Exploitation Plan** describes how your projected sales will be achieved, in the short to mid-term. Ideas without action are meaningless. Take your vision, break it down into smaller incremental goals and attack the objectives as if your life depends on it. This section builds on the earlier market research and analysis conducted for the situation paragraph. By defining your market and outlining your targeted segments and their buyer behavior, you the business leader, have the ability to construct an action oriented approach to attacking markets.

The exploitation plan takes advantage of the critical vulnerability in the market. It describes the initial go to market strategy and short-term growth strategy focused toward flourishing in the long term. Landing in a smaller market and expanding outside of that initial market by saturating, and ultimately, monopolizing it. Expansion out of the initial market shows progress toward accomplishing the goal of competing at the 'center of gravity' in your industry. Exploiting an objective for the betterment of the greater initiative. Determining that action which may result in the greatest value for the given situation then committing to action. That's the beauty of the "5 Paragraph Business Plan".

3.   Exploitation Plan; go to market, growth strategy.
- Marketing strategy – "customer-centric".
  o   Overall marketing strategy.
  o   Pricing.
- Sales strategy – experience based.
  o   The selling cycle.
  o   Sales tactics.
  o   Distribution.
- Promotion strategy.
  o   Advertising and sale promotions.
  o   Publicity.
- Customer service/ support.
  o   Warranty or guarantee policies.
4.   Desired End State.
- Satisfied customer.
- Returning customer.
- Brand ambassadors.
- Breakeven chart and calculation.
- **Profit durability.**

Timelines

Every mission has a deadline. There may be an expiration date associated with your market or your entire organization. Time management is essential when conducting business. Create phases to help breakdown the large-scale time elements into to smaller, more manageable blocks. Start by looking at the long-term objectives of your overall organization. This may be a 3-5-year view at the overall market landscape, drawing assumptions from many different resources. Break the years down by quarters and begin segmenting the quarters by objective and team assignments. Objectives that are routine in nature may be associated with the continual function of the business such as human resources, payroll, accounting etc. The priority timelines are based on quota or expiring deals, rates, discounts, crop yields etc., causing a sense of urgency. Outside forces, natural occurrences, nefarious actors, these are all potential risks to your business and may need to be handled at an unforeseen moment. Plan, as best you can, for the unknown and assign teams to handle those actionable timelines that need immediate attention.

---

* METT-**T**SL - **T**ime Available: Actionable, Priority, Routine.
The overall timeline and objective timelines to be executed are worked through in the business plan. The "5 Paragraph Business Plan" is a living document that requires adjustment after each pivot is made throughout the mission timeline.

Objective timelines focus on the enabling components of the plan. They fall into 3 basic categories in the order of most urgent to least urgent.

Actionable timelines are based on an urgent situation that requires immediate attention. They generally, take teams off their original task and throw everyone into chaos. Thoughtful prior planning and developed processes enable team leadership to implement strategies necessary to mitigate risk in the moment and prevent future risk from occurring. This puts the lowest level employee in the decision maker's spot. With a properly filled out "5 Paragraph Business Plan", subordinate leaders are empowered to commit action. Actionable timelines involve objectives that must be accomplished before another can take place. They may involve unforeseen elements such as effects of the environment or stolen property. Outside influences affecting the business.

An example would be, if a shipment is being held up and the customer *NEEDS* the item ASAP, there must be a process and team assigned to that task – a reaction team, for example. This should be planned for in advance to prevent any additional lag in the supply chain. The assigned team performs a primary role within the company knowing that they could be tasked in case something happens. Prove to your team and potential investors that you have carefully thought through the risks associated with working in the industry and provide a plan for how to handle the unexpected. Empower your leaders.

Priority timelines need to happen for an operation to occur smoothly. These are the important elements that fall within the timeline of a planned event. Priority timelines have deadlines and expectations attached to them. This could be a running calendar used by project managers who task subordinate teams to complete planned mission objectives. These timelines provide scope to the overall mission with multiple priority timelines that occur systematically within them.

Routine timelines illustrate the daily continuous operations that are necessary for the business to function. They are routine but they are vital to the overall venture. Mostly associated with the fixed overhead costs.

B. Concept of the Operations

    5. Scheme of Maneuver
- Overall economic model.
- Marketing plan.
- Walk through what it should look like when executing the plan.
- All moving parts are assigned a task, conditions and, standards.

The marketing plan needs to provide scope and detail to the overall marketing strategy that will exploit the opportunity by employing your competitive advantages. Be sure to include sales and service policies, pricing, distribution, promotion and advertising strategies, and sales projections. The marketing plan needs to describe what needs to be done, how it will be done, when it will be done, and who will do it.

    6. Design & Development Plan
- Development status and tasks.
- Difficulties and risks.
- Product improvement and new products.
- Costs.
- Proprietary issues: ownership of patents, trademarks, copyright etc.
  - Emergency roles – basic processes for handling crisis.
  - Lowest level leadership.

Companies who are working in design mode, i.e. non-existent products, doing research and development or have technical obstacles to overcome, or working on intellectual property rights, etc. this portion of the plan is extremely important. However, if you are in a business that does not require research and development (e.g., retail goods, consumables) you can skip this section and just discuss any technologies you plan to employ during operations.

Describe in detail the full extent of any design and development work that needs to be considered. List the cost and time required before the product or service is ready for market. Often, design and development costs are underestimated. Be sure to backup all costs with market research. "It's better to underpromise and overdeliver." Design and development includes the engineering work necessary to construct a prototype and bring it to a finished product; the design of specialty tooling; industrial design work; marketing design to make a product more attractive; equipment, and special techniques and the employees who are capable of such skilled labor that may be required.

C. Tasks
- Delegation of authority – assumption of responsibility.
- Priority based on market variables [point of friction].
  - Research and development, sales, marketing, business development, strategic partnerships, warehouse setup etc.

Coordinating Instructions; Operations Plan

Outline how your business will function and deliver value to your customers. Operations, as defined, is the process to deliver your goods/ products/ services to a customer or user. This includes the production process for delivering your service to a given customer, your manufacturing process (if you are a manufacturer), transportation, logistics, travel, printing, consulting, and after-sales service. It also includes factors such as manufacturing plant location, the type of facilities needed, space requirements, internal processes, capital equipment requirements, and labor force; both fulltime and part-time requirements.

For a processing business, the processing and operations plan needs to include policies on how to handle inventory, purchasing of supplies, process control, and which parts of the process are outsourced, what must be purchased, and which operations will be performed by your internal workforce broken down into teams.

Location specific businesses such as service businesses or a retail business may require additional reconnaissance to determine proximity to customers and time of typical purchase. Every system within the operation must be laid out; the service delivery or merchandising system, methods for minimizing overhead, and how the company will obtain competitive productivity from a labor force.

Compromises from operations to expenses must be discussed. For instance, an operation may take a significant amount of time in the beginning because you are performing the task yourself as you search for a qualified person to fulfill the role within the company. Long term success comes with refining your operations and processes. This is where you show how you will measure results in order to manage the overall business effectively.

D. Coordinating Instructions; Operations Plan

- Operating model and cycle.
- Operations strategy.
- Geographic location.
- Facilities, equipment and, improvements.
- Capacity levels and inventory management & control.
- Legal issues affecting operations.
  - Identify key leadership.
  - Role of leadership.
    - Teams.
    - Role of team members.
      - Gear specific to team member.
      - Equipment specific to mission.
      - Additional specific consideration.

Paragraph 4: Admin/Logistics – Progress, Milestones, the "ASK"

Present a '30,000 foot' visual timeline of your company. Show the progress made thus far and future events along the path to mission success. Highlight major events and the interrelationship of your company's major alliances with other businesses (under the 'Situation-Friendly') and their necessary involvement to launch the venture and achieve objectives quintessential to success of the business. The overall operating cycle and cash conversion methods of the business will provide key variables for readers to focus on in the schedule and timeline. Often, entrepreneurs and business leaders underestimate the time necessary to complete tasks and deliver objectives. Deadlines are critical to a venture's success. It is important to demonstrate that you have correctly estimated the timelines for each objective in determining the schedule. A well thought out schedule presented in a precise timeline can be an extremely valuable tool in convincing team members of your vision, and to prove to potential investors that you and your team are capable and responsible individuals.

A. Administration – Basic Business Functions
- Highlights of the financial statements.
- Cost controls.
- Human resources - employee management.
- Employment and other agreements, stock options and bonus plans.
- Documents to be developed for this section (put financial statements in appendix).
- Pro forma income statements.
- Pro forma balance sheets.
- Pro forma cash flow analysis.

FINANCIAL PLAN (create 5 years of pro forma statements; put them in the appendix)
Every business has risk and financial hurdles to face. In this portion of the "5 Paragraph Business Plan" you must collect all the market research and combine it with the intelligence you've gathered from other industry resources to create pro forma. Pro forma means; to produce as a matter of form or politeness. It's a fancy way of saying make it all up. Grasp for straws. Make assumptions…. and back them up with factual evidence compiled into a neat concise manner. You must create your own documents and spreadsheets that illustrate the opportunity hypothesis you have based your vision on.

Describe all the risks and the consequences associated with those risks should a negative outcome occur. Discuss the risks to the industry, your company, and the personnel within the company - given the market appeal of your product, and the timing and financing of your venture. Include assumptions concerning your sales projections, purchase orders, order fulfillments and so on. Don't be afraid to highlight the potential fatal flaw within your venture. Acknowledging that it may be an issue shows maturity. Provide solutions for how the situation will be handled should the need arise. These smaller plans within the larger "5 Paragraph

Business Plan" are called FRAG-Os or fragmentary orders. They are simply smaller versions of the greater plan but, in some cases, may include more zoomed-in detail for a given problem. Each one is a small action plan in case of an urgent situation that may require an actionable timeline, which an assigned team will potentially carry out. Fragmentary orders are great tools to have as a manager. We will discuss FRAG-Os later in the book.

Essentially, you are proving that you're aware of the obstacles facing your business. You are aware of the reality that businesses fail. Highlight the main threats facing your business, based on your assumptions. Show how you will avoid or overcome them. Failure to recognize important risks and mitigate their effect can degrade the overall success of the venture. Don't let this be the determining factor preventing your company from getting financed, or your project from getting funded. Be aware of the potential challenges that lay ahead. Prove to everyone that you are taking the long look at your venture and improving every step of the way.

It is often the case that potential financiers prioritize this portion of the "5 Paragraph Business Plan". Be thorough and make sure you put sufficient effort toward explaining the financials of your business. In order to run a successful business, you must be thorough in your understanding of the financials pertaining to the venture. You do not want people to think you are naïve or lackadaisical about the current situation of your business. Not being forthcoming may cause someone to get the impression you are nefarious or malicious in your actions. That will surely lose the faith of a would-be investor or potential business partner. This is where you demonstrate your skills as a manager. Take the initiative and prove that you have thought about the risks and can handle them. By identifying and discussing the risks in your venture you increase your own credibility and the overall business venture. That puts a great deal of ease to the minds of potential investors or other stakeholders.

Highlights of the Financial Statements
In this portion of the "5 Paragraph Business Plan" showcase the highlights of your financial statements. This section paints a picture of the overall financial performance of the business during the various phases as it is started, stabilizes and grows. The financial plan is the foundation for evaluating an investment opportunity. It represents your best estimate of the financial requirements your business needs to meet in order to be successful. The purpose of the financial plan is to provide team members, potential investors or stakeholders with a clear understanding of the venture's financial potential and worth in the long term by presenting a timetable for financial viability. By providing financial milestones this plan may also serve as a timeline and an operating plan for financial management. Consider writing a fragmentary order, within the financial plan, outlining the milestones discussed and how each FRAG-O combines to create a long-term operational plan.

This is where you need to think creatively as a business planner. Think about creative cost saving measures that can be utilized to reach the next stage of growth. For instance, bootstrapping techniques, to get the startup venture rolling, especially in the early stages of business. Highlight the important conclusions based upon earlier assumptions such as; what is the maximum amount of capital required to make entry into the market, and when is it required? If you are working with debt to create your company, what is the amount needed? When do you expect to pay it off? What is your amortization strategy for paying off the debt? The strategies and assumptions discussed earlier provide clarity as to when the venture will attain a positive cash flow and if, or when, you will run out of cash; requiring more debt or fund raising through equity investment. Through analysis, you may determine there is another, more enticing, critical vulnerability or target market.

Point out every significant milestone in cash flow that will occur as you grow and are capable of adding capacity. With your entry strategy, marketing plan, sales projections and proposed financing - what do you estimate it will take to reach a unit breakeven sales level? How many months to breakeven? Provide the assumed sales and profit performance patterns over time given external forces such as environment and seasons. Compare critical financial ratios from your plan with other business' ratios found in your industry, then explain and justify significant differences. This validates your plan by comparison.

Cost Controls

Describe your methods for gathering reported costs information and how often those key metrics are monitored, as well as who is responsible for controlling the various cost elements. Describe what actions will be taken if (and when) the budget overruns. Explain any unusual items that were not identified in the financial statement.

Prove the potential financial feasibility of your new venture with organized pro forma and by showing a plan for creating profit. The management team must monitor cash flow by forecasting financial operating needs; such as equipment or other assets. Startup ventures with low capital reserves must closely monitor the outflow and inflow of cash on a short-term basis. Furthermore, pro forma balance sheets are a detailed collection of the assets required to support the projected level of operations necessary to make the projected growth milestones. Through liabilities it shows how these assets are going to be financed. All of this is combined into projected balance sheets, which can indicate if there is sufficient working capital given the projected debt-to-equity ratios. To justify future financing for the venture or project the working capital, current ratios, inventory turnover and the like, all need to be within acceptable limits. These limits are situationally dependent. They are based on industry standards, market limitations, investor propensity to accept risk etc. Work with advisors and mentors to build a strong pro forma financial picture of your company.

Pro Forma Income Statements

Prepare pro forma income statements (also referred to as profit & loss statements) using the operating costs and sales forecasts for the first 3 years and create potential projections. Use these assumptions to predict growth beyond that point.

Make sure that your data is consistent with what you discussed in the other sections of the "5 Paragraph Business Plan", such as the marketing strategy, concept of operations, management team, etc. Fully discuss the assumptions made preparing the pro forma income statement and document them; you may want to cite them in detail and make a note (e.g., general and administrative costs being a fixed percentage of costs or sales, the amount of bad debts and discounts that is allowed, or any assumptions made with respect to sales expenses as a portion of cost of goods sold or the sales budget) many of these types of assumptions require additional explanation and detail. Highlight the major risks that could prevent the venture's sales and profit goals from being attained, and the importance of the risks to the projected profits. Acknowledge the risks in the pro forma and build a planned strategy to mitigate those risks while growing income.

Pro Forma Balance Sheets
Given what you've learned thus far, create pro forma balance sheets for the beginning of the year and the end of the year, for the first 3 years of operation.

Pro Forma Cash Flow Analysis
Cash flows are projected monthly for the first year of operation. They're projected quarterly for at least the next two years of growth. By detailing the amount of cash on hand and the requirements and limitations for working capital; and the timing of expected cash inflows and outflows you can determine the need for additional financing and the timeframe in which it may be required. If additional financing is to be obtained, such as bank loans, or short-term lines of credit from banks, or through equity financing -Outline the terms of credit and how it is intended to be repaid.

This is based on cash, not accrual, accounting. Show them how much money you will need.

What will you use as collateral for debt funding? How will the money be used; for working capital, design & development of the product, marketing & sales, advertising, capital acquisitions? Investors generally feel that cost associated with design & development and marketing are riskier than are expenditures for capital acquisitions. These various elements help determine the investment's level of risk and aid in the investors assessment of the company. Discuss how cash flow sensitivity plays a role in the business functions within your company. (e.g., possible changes in such crucial assumptions such as achieving lower sales than was forecasted, an increase in the receivable collection period, or an increase in the cost of vital manufacturing components). Discuss assumptions, such as the timing of collection of receivables, trade discounts given (bartering services with mutual value), planned salary and wage increases, anticipated increases in any operating expenses, terms of payments to your vendors, inventory turnovers per year, seasonality characteristics of the business as they affect inventory requirements, capital equipment purchases etc. This is your opportunity to outline where all the dollars and cents go. Again, this is a - CASH - analysis, not accrual.

Break-Even Analysis

Conduct a breakeven analysis to determine the target level of production and sales necessary to become profitable. Business leaders use this analysis to calculate the number of units that need to be sold in order for the company to turn a profit. Alternatively, they use this analysis to determine the level of sales in dollars that needs to be met for the company to become profitable. You will need to calculate the total fixed costs in order to determine the contribution margin and contribution margin ratio. Then use that information to determine the break-even point. Fixed costs are constant costs, such as rent or a long-term lease, depreciation, salaries, insurance etc. They are independent of business activity and otherwise known as "overhead" or "fixed overhead costs". The contribution margin refers to an individual product being sold. It is the amount of revenue collected from selling each product. The contribution margin ratio is the percentage of revenue that is going toward fixed costs. This illustrates the point where revenue and costs meet for a given product or revenue stream. This ratio also demonstrates the balance between growth and sustainability for a product line or an entire company. Each product has a contribution margin and a contribution margin ratio associated with it. When compiled, each product joins the product line, which comprises the revenue stream within a market. Multiple revenue streams within a target market, and further growth into broader markets, generates more capital and increases sustainability and long-term growth.

The following formulas contribute to the break-even analysis:

Sale price: cost to the customer at retail.

Variable cost: all costs associated with producing, selling, and distribution; raw materials, labor, sales force, energy consumption etc.

Contribution margin = sale price - variable cost to create the individual product

Contribution margin ratio for a product = contribution margin / sale price

Contribution margin ratio for a revenue stream = contribution margin / revenue

Break-even point in sales = Fixed costs / contribution margin ratio

Break-even point in units = Fixed costs / contribution margin (of a single unit)

The break-even point, in sales and in units, is used to build your timeline for return on investment in the long term. Use the break-even analysis, sales projections, and market research regarding seasonal sales trends and target customer behavior to construct a vision for how your company will work toward profitability. Ultimately, you are showing how you are going to make a return on investment.

Commonly Used Terms and Formulas

Revenue: Income gained through business activity.

Cost of goods sold: Cost of materials and direct labor needed to produce the goods.

Gross margin = total sales revenue – cost of goods sold.

Gross profit = total revenue – cost of goods sold.

Operating profit: Profit earned through the main functions of the business. This does not include earnings made through outside investments.

Asset: A physical resource which retains a standard economic value. Corporations, organizations, countries or an individual may own or control assets with the intent of reaping future benefit from them.

Liability: Debt or financial obligations that are settled over an established period of time. Liabilities occur naturally throughout the course of doing business.

> **Shareholders Equity = Total Assets - Total Liabilities.**
> **Balance Sheet Formula:** Assets = Liabilities + Shareholder's Equity.

Earnings retained: NET earnings that are kept by the company to be reinvested. These earnings are not to be distributed as dividends. Located on the balance sheet under shareholders' equity.

Dividend: A portion of the company's earnings that will be distributed to the shareholders. Dividend distribution is typically associated with a profitability timeline showing the breakeven threshold. Once a company has broken even, and become profitable, it may be decided by the board of directors or key ownership to pay out dividends to company shareholders.

Growth rate: Projected earning potential over the long term. Once a company has broken even, and become profitable, it may be decided by the board of directors or key ownership to pay out dividends to company shareholders. The annualized percentage of growth over a given period of time, typically 5 years. To determine the growth rate, project 5 years of sales, then take each year's dividend and divide it by the previous year's dividend minus 1.

> **Growth rate formula =** current year dividend / (previous year dividend - 1)
> Yr. 1 - 100
> Yr. 2 - 103 -- 103 / 100 - 1 = 3%
> Yr. 3 - 108 -- 108 / 103 - 1 = 4.85%
> Yr. 4 - 110 -- 110 / 108 - 1 = 1.85%
> Yr. 5 - 125 -- 125 / 110 - 1 = 13.6%

YoY: Year over Year   **QoQ**: Quarter over Quarter.

ROE: Return on Equity = growth rate / earnings retained.

ROA: Return on Assets = NET income / total assets.

ROI: Return on Investment = investment revenue - investment cost / investment cost.

EBIT: Earnings Before Interest and Taxes (cash flow prior to debt).

EBITDA: Earnings Before Interest Taxes and Amortization (cash flow given debt).

Developing the Documentation

The pro forma you've created so far is the bedrock needed to create professional financial exhibits. Creating pro forma for the financial plan can be intimidating. Do not hesitate to consult with an accountant if you need assistance. Your accountant will appreciate any work you've done so far. The more detail you provide in these exhibits, the more enticing they may appear to investors or stakeholders. Prove to the onlooker that you have thought through all the conceivable objectives and potential outcomes and consulted with professionals. **Make it a struggle to challenge your assumptions.**

Pro forma you the owner or business leader need to prepare; and present to an accounting professional:

- Pro forma [3-5 years] monthly income statements (for at least the first 1-2 years).
- Pro forma [3-5 years] balance sheets.
- Pro forma [3-5 years] cash flow analysis (for at least the first 1-2 years).

Use real-time cash flow analysis of expected receipts and disbursements to estimate cash flow needs. This cash-based analysis provides a more accurate picture than an accrual-based, accounting. The analysis you've made of the operating and cash conversion cycle will enable you to identify critical assumptions. Specify in your attached exhibits all your assumptions behind items such as inventory requirements, cost of goods sold, sales levels, payable periods, collections and overall growth. Once you've compiled all the information required, attach all financial statements to the appendix of your business plan.

ASK - The Proposed Company Offering

You have shown what you are going to do with the money, here is where you ask for the exact amount of capital you need; while providing what your company/team is offering in order to receive the capital such as equity, shares, equipment, product, services etc. that which is necessary to complete the mission.

This portion of the "5 Paragraph Business Plan" indicates the amount of any money that is needed to start the venture, what securities are being offered to the investor, followed by a brief description as to how the capital will be used and a summary of how the business will achieve the investor's targeted rate of return.

This is only the initial step toward successfully negotiating the terms associated with investments. Be prepared for a high degree of scrutiny put toward your plan and management team. There may be several levels of due diligence and interviews that take place prior to an investment being made or a project getting approved.

Your entire "5 Paragraph Business Plan" will back-up this ASK.

- Desired financing.
- Offering (this is the deal structure your pitch for money).
- Capitalization.
- Use of funds.
- Investor's return (exit strategy).

Exit strategy: Investors and business leaders typically execute this strategy when an investment or business venture has met its profit objective. An exit strategy may also be considered as a contingency plan that is executed by an investor, venture capitalist, business leader, or business owner. It is the act of liquidating one's position in an asset or company, once certain criteria are met or exceeded. Reasons for executing an exit strategy may include; exiting a company that has not met performance standards or closing a business, or business segment, that is not generating profits.

B. Logistics – The Moving Parts Associated with Routine Business

- Supply chain management.
- Construction.
- Transportation.
- Inventory management.
- Warehouse management.
- Customer care.
- Hospitality.
  ---etc.
- Additional logistics concerns associated with your business.
  - o All moving parts imperative to accomplishing specific objectives.
  - o Include contingencies for emergency situations.

Adjacent units: In the situation paragraph, we discuss the potential in leveraging your organization's value in order to achieve mission success. The value that you offer is wrapped up your mission statement and directives along with the goods or services that you provide. Consider working with adjacent units to alleviate costly expenses. You can achieve more by eliminating costs through structured relationships. Exchanging value rather than currency still requires a contract. Be sure to structure your relationship and hold one another accountable.

---

* METT-TSL: Space/ Logistics: Building a capital runway, growth assumptions, and sustainment plan are keys to running a successful business. Where will you be operating and how will you maintain operations? Roughly translated, how big is the market and what are your capital runway, growth assumptions and sustainment plans?

Paragraph 5: Command/Signal – Company Leadership, Customer Care

This portion of the "5 Paragraph Business Plan" includes key descriptions of each function within the organization and what expertise are needed to fill that specific role. Included is a background for each of the vital management personnel and their primary duties and responsibilities pertaining to their role. Provide an outline of the organizational structure and how the components operate to grow the venture. Include a biography of the board of directors and key advisors along with a description of their role and the importance it has on mission success. Include a description for the position of each owner and the position of any other investors or shareholders; whomever owns equity within the company. You must present a solid commitment of efforts from everyone involved in the key roles crucial to business success; team members, board members, advisors, investors etc.

You must prove that the management team is capable and responsible for the planning and execution of all business functions. Provide understanding as to how the team is balanced between technical expertise, managerial experience and overall business acumen. Provide background on you and your team members as to why you are able to recognize hurdles and minimize investor risk; and prove that you are capable of breaking down the hurdles your venture is facing, thus leading to the overall growth of the venture and a profitable return for everyone involved.

A. **Signal; Communication to Leadership and "Go-To" Processes for Given Scenarios**
Provide the physical address of your company and the methods for contacting leaders at your company.

Primary – *Email.*
Alternate - *Private message, chat, or instant message.*
Contingency - *Text message.*
Emergency – *Phone.*

B. **Command; Management Team**
Location of Key Leaders - *address, title, contact information.*
   - Primary work location.
   - Primary method of communication.
Succession of Command - *hierarchy of authority & responsibility.*
   - Organization structure.
   - Key management and personnel within the organization structure.
   - Management compensation and equity ownership.
   - Other current investors.
   - Board of directors or board of advisors.
      o Other shareholders, rights and, restrictions.

Develop a formal board of directors and a formal advisory board based on the needs of your organization. It is important to have an appropriate size board to fit your organization. Keep in mind that board members actively work toward the success of the organization. They can be shareholders or associated with your organization by other means. The point is, they are interested in the overall success of the venture. Typically, board members are prominent business leaders, entrepreneurs, investors, private equity, trusts etc. Their connections and overall network should be leveraged for the betterment of the organization.

---

* **METT-TSL: Team & Support**: The command paragraph describes the management team that is directly responsible for the daily operations of the business. Each member of the team plays a critical role in the success of the overall mission. Outline the team in your METT-TSL template. Include their name, title credentials, title, description of the role they play and how it pertains to mission success.

Signal				
Primary				
Alternate				
Contingent				
Emergency				

Command	Location of Key Leaders			
Address				
Email				

Orientation – Executive Summary

It's time to complete the plan using the **METT-TSL** template. The orientation paragraph or 'Executive Summary' is the last section that you write in a business plan. It is the first thing every reader sees when reading through your plan. The 'Executive Summary' summarizes the true essence of your business in a concise manner. Each area of the plan is briefly highlighted along with the operational leader designated to accomplish the outlined objectives. This is based on the decisions made by the executive leadership who are responsible for overall mission success. Each operational leader is given authority over the operational element that falls within their expertise, which is crucial for mission success. This orientation paragraph is not simply a "small" business plan but rather, it highlights the problem / opportunity for the reader and provides the vision and scope of the business. The reader must be enticed by the opportunity and encouraged to read more.

This is where you *sell* the vision of your business to team members, customers, potential investors, and stakeholders. Often time entrepreneurs and business leaders fail to consider the true adequacy of their markets, the customers they are targeting and a structured business model that will enable them to accomplish their mission and achieve success. They get engrossed by creating a piece of technology or struggle to deliver a product, which is not the same thing as delivering an attractive business opportunity. The executive summary encourages the reader to continue through the situation paragraph to gain a broader understanding of the problem/opportunity, and on to the mission statement to learn what your company aims to provide as a valuable solution. Remember, the mission statement and directives encourage the reader to ask, "HOW are they going to do that?", leading them further toward the execution paragraph and framing up the 'ASK'. This plays out like a story by keeping the reader interested throughout the text.

These questions will help you focus on the crucial aspects of your executive summary that will help entice readers to read further into the details of your business plan.

> **What is your company's mission?**
> **What is your enemy - who is your target market and what problem do they face?**
> **Who is on your team - what role do they play / what functions are outsourced?**
> **What environment are you in- is your business seasonal - what do you do to mitigate effects?**
> **How long have you been working on this - when do you expect to present a product and launch?**
> **What type of space does your business require; brick & mortar, online, transit etc.?**
> **What are the functioning components of the business - what do they need to make the business a success?**

These are the elements of METT-TSL. (You were filling out the template, right?) Now fill out your executive summary by answering these basic questions on the METT-TSL template.

- Problem-Opportunity Statement.
- Description of the Target Market.
- Business Concept and Product or Service.
- Technology and Operational Issues.
- Economics.
- Financial Highlights.
- Financial Need.
- The Team.
- Contact Information.

The Orientation - executive summary is often the first, and only thing a reader looks through. You must summarize the business in a comprehensive, clear, concise way that is well written. Show your VALUE in the beginning by highlighting the true pain that your customers are actively dealing with and how you will crush that pain by providing the solution to their problems. With this template and the "5 Paragraph Business Plan" you are able to construct a clear and concise image of your business vision. Enticing team members, customers or would be investors to follow your sound vision and focus.

Mission
Who, What, When, Where, Why
- The Company and Concept.
- The Product and or Service.
- Entry and Growth Strategy.

VALUE that you are offering.

Enemy – the problem, the *NEED or demand* (*problem you will solve*
Summarize the industry in which the proposed business will operate.

Industry/Market
- Discuss briefly industry size (in Dollars) and annual growth rate (%).
- Discuss the structure of the industry at present.

Size, Activity, Location, Uniform, Time, Equipment

Center of Gravity, Critical Vulnerability, Exploitation Plan
- Market segmentation and target market.
- Estimated market share and sales figures.

Enemy's Assumed Course of Action; Market Analysis
- Discuss assumptions implicit in the plan.
- Identify and discuss any major problems and other risks.
- Address assumptions/potential problems/risks critical to the success of the venture.

Team & Support
Size of the team; 4, 12, 42.
Capabilities, Features, Unfair Advantage
- Organization.
- Key management and personnel.
- Management compensation and ownership.
- Other current investors.
- Employment and other agreements, stock options and, bonus plans.
- Board of directors or board of advisors.
- Other shareholders, rights and, restrictions.
- Supporting professional advisors and services.

Terrain & Weather
General Location; Environmental Conditions, Seasonal Dependents, Geography

Time
Schedule until market - 3-6-9-month projection; 3-5-year growth strategy
- Current trends [3-6 months].
- Long term trends [2-5 years].
- Provide standard financial ratios for the industry.

Space
Development Iterations – [seen obstacles to success].

Logistics
Barriers to Entry; Capital, Equipment, Transportation, Technology...etc.

Using the "5 Paragraph Business Plan" as an Operational Leader

Business plan creators must disseminate their plan to members of the management team and every individual based upon their function in the organization. Each operational leader with a management role must be identified in the overall plan. Each operational leader must then take key elements from the large-scale plan to produce their own smaller scale "5 Paragraph Business Plan". The operational plans are more detailed than the overall plan. Operational leaders should include the details of each team leader and the members of their teams; include the team role and individual assigned roles and the duties and responsibilities pertaining to the assigned role. Everyone on the team must be assigned a role including, and especially, the leader. This method of planning maintains accountability between everyone on the team, from front to back.

Operational Leaders

Given the information from the executive leadership's higher overall plan, the operational leader constructs their own "5 Paragraph Business Plan". Every significant function and critical phase of the venture needs a separate operational plan. Orders are given to conduct operations based on these, more detailed, operational plans. Note how and why this may differ from higher command's plan. Notice how the many segments of the executive leadership's overall "5 Paragraph Business Plan" fit into the operational leader's plan. The 'enemy' or situation/opportunity statement and coordinating instructions directly carries over into the operational plan. Operational leaders use specific elements of the overall mission and execution paragraphs to construct a situation paragraph for your internal team. Your primary focus as an operational leader is on the "Execution" paragraph.

Operational leaders are tasked based upon the functions found within the overall execution paragraph. It is up to you as the operational leader to create your own 'commander's intent' based on the mission, the values, and ethics of the overall organization. Detail the concept of operations, as you see it. Tell executive leadership what you see the operation looking like with all the key elements working smoothly. Describe what a "perfect operation" would look like. Create the scheme of maneuver for the elements put under your charge. Provide details for the design/development needs that you may have as an operational component within the overall plan. Outline key tasks and the personnel assigned to fulfill the roles pertaining to those tasks. Carry over the exact coordinating instructions from executive leadership's overall plan. Drawing upon elements of the overall, executive leadership plan, provide coordinating instructions for your operational team. These instructions may include timelines and phases that need to be completed by another operational team prior to meeting the overall objective.

Operational leaders use executive leader's admin/logistics and command/signal paragraphs in in your operational plans. Space & Logistics is provided by executive leadership. The space refers to the location and the dimensions of the workspace. This may include the geographic area(s) and/or the environment you'll be operating in, a diagram of a brick and mortar structure, or an event layout. The logistics is provided by support elements. These support elements are part of the larger overall company. It is assumed when using the "5 Paragraph Business Plan" that executive leadership is providing guidance to operational leadership by filling in a complete 'Admin/Logistics paragraph'. It is important for executive leadership to provide operational leadership with a broad understanding of the overall company situation, mission, an overview of the execution, commander's intent and desired end state. Operational leadership must have a clear understanding of the overall concept of operations and how their team fits into the scheme of maneuver. They need to have a clear understanding of the layout of the space they'll be operating in and the logistical support that will be offered by the larger company.

The intent of the following diagram is to show you where the elements of METT-TSL fit within the overall plan. Use this guidebook along with the METT-TSL template to construct your team's operational "5 Paragraph Business plan".

"5 Paragraph Business Plan"
METT-TSL Flowchart

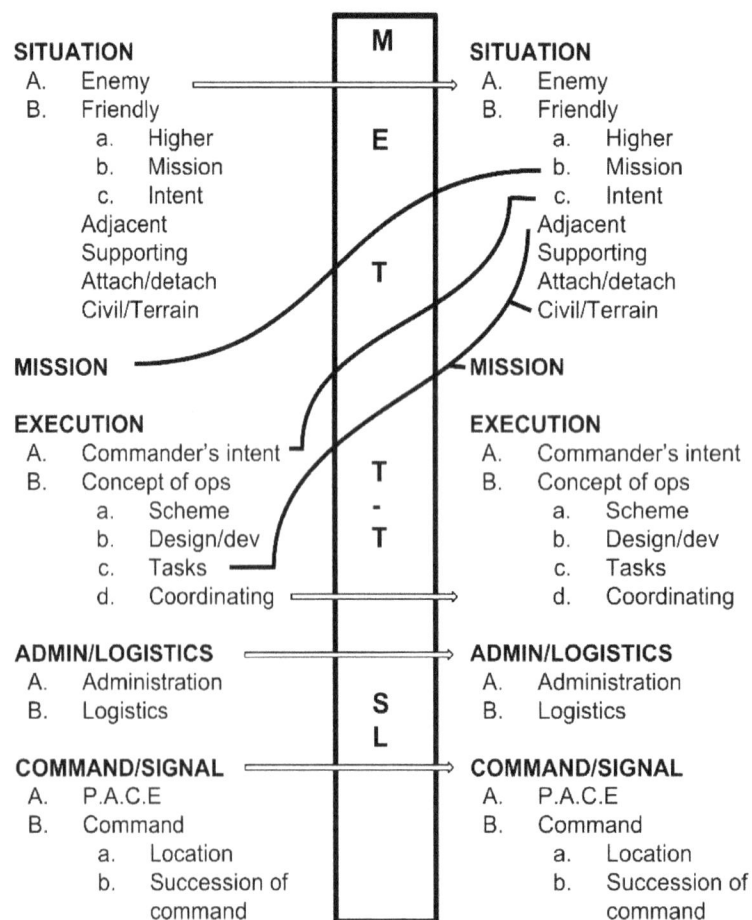

SITUATION	M	SITUATION
A. Enemy		A. Enemy
B. Friendly		B. Friendly
a. Higher	E	a. Higher
b. Mission		b. Mission
c. Intent		c. Intent
Adjacent		Adjacent
Supporting		Supporting
Attach/detach	T	Attach/detach
Civil/Terrain		Civil/Terrain
MISSION		**MISSION**
EXECUTION		**EXECUTION**
A. Commander's intent		A. Commander's intent
B. Concept of ops	T	B. Concept of ops
a. Scheme	-	a. Scheme
b. Design/dev	T	b. Design/dev
c. Tasks		c. Tasks
d. Coordinating		d. Coordinating
ADMIN/LOGISTICS		**ADMIN/LOGISTICS**
A. Administration	S	A. Administration
B. Logistics	L	B. Logistics
COMMAND/SIGNAL		**COMMAND/SIGNAL**
A. P.A.C.E		A. P.A.C.E
B. Command		B. Command
a. Location		a. Location
b. Succession of command		b. Succession of command

Using the "5 Paragraph Business Plan to Conduct an Operation

FRAG-O: Fragmentary Order

It is up to you the operational leader to take charge and carry out their operational "5 Paragraph Business Plan" as approved by executive leadership. ALL personnel must be briefed the overall plan and the more detailed operational plan pertaining to their specific business function within the organization. Key personnel, such as team leaders, construct a fragmentary order for their team's role in the company's overall operational plan. A fragmentary order or FRAG-O (pronounced FRaay-Go), is based on the operational leader's "5 Paragraph Business Plan". Simply put, a FRAG-O is a less detailed, miniature, operational plan and pertains ONLY to a specific objective or task. Every objective within the significant functions of the organization must have a FRAG-O. Key elements are taken from the operational "5 Paragraph Business Plan" and used to create FRAG-Os for teams to operate in a direct action. FRAG-Os may be created 'on-the-fly' based on the needs of the operation. Use FRAG-Os when operating on an 'actionable' timeline. They are a quick effective way to execute a task and accomplish objectives.

"5 Paragraph Business Plan" - Fragmentary Order

Operational Leader:

Coordinator:	**Date:**
Team - Section:	**Task Organization:**
Team Leader:	**Team Members:**

Capabilities/Limitations:

Objective/Task:

Situation

Problem to solve.
Friendlies in the area who can help.

Mission

Task; who will accomplish, what needs to be done, where it needs to be done, when it will be executed, in order to…. accomplish X [WHY?].

Execution

Commander's intent; ethically completing the mission while adding value.
Potential method for accomplishing the task.
Coordinating instructions to leadership.
Desired end goal- what life looks like with the solution.

Support Plan

Additional special equipment, added personnel – utilize for solving the problem

Command/Signal

Coordinator of events, Who the key leaders are, How the key leaders communicate, how you get in touch with leadership.

Fragmentary orders, FRAG-Os, are extremely important. Your business plan is a *living document* that needs to be updated from time to time. A great deal of effort is put into creating your overall "5 Paragraph Business Plan" and operational plans. Ask key leaders within your operational team to create FRAG-Os based on situations that may arise through standard business operations. These FRAG-Os can be reused based on recurring situations and may be the key to finding areas of improvement within your business operations. Use FRAG-Os to update your operational plan and overall plan. Empower your leadership within the organization. FRAG-Os result in actions, which require debriefs. Debriefs are a chance for everyone to provide the intelligence they gathered as individuals into an after action review. After action reviews are used to improve your overall plan and could be the key to succeeding in the long run. Intelligence goes both ways in business: from executive leadership briefing the overall vision and disseminating information - to operators in the field committing to action, gathering intelligence and reporting that intelligence to the executive level to be used when making long term decisions.

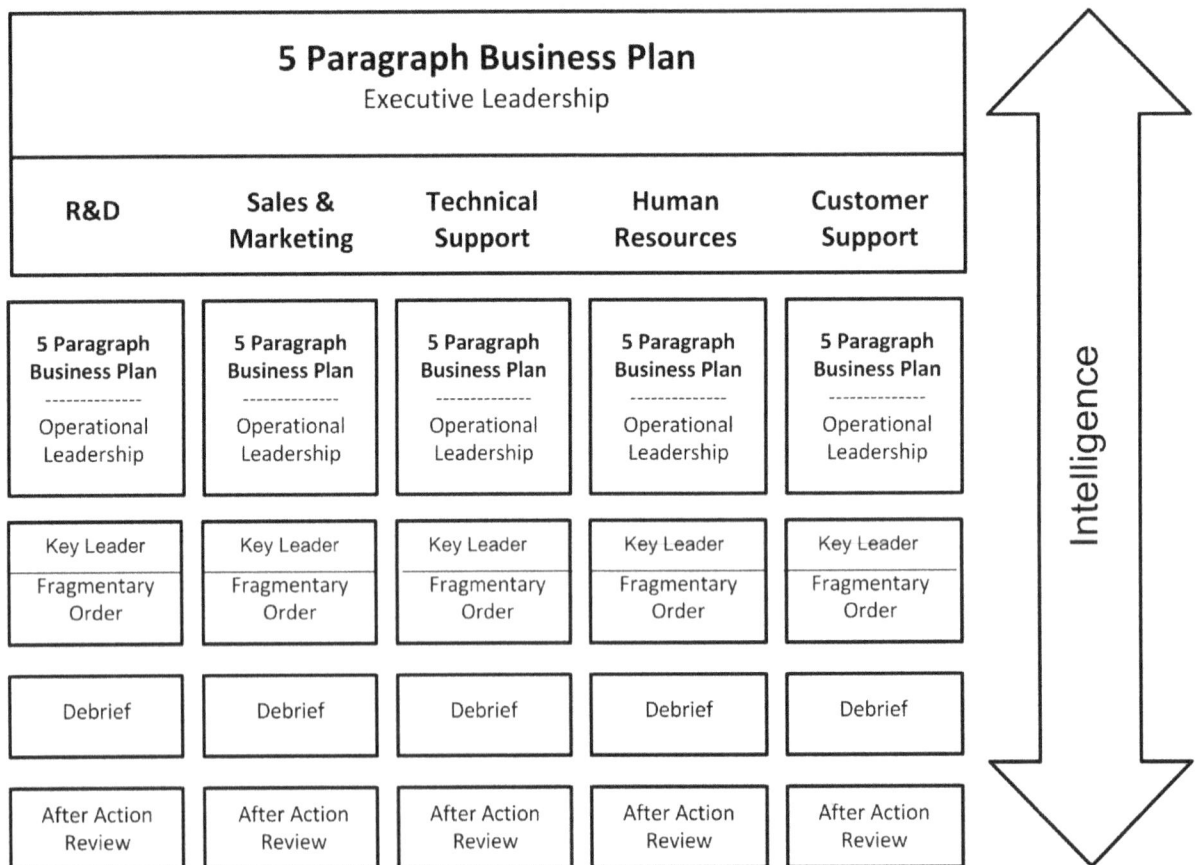

5 Paragraph Business Plan				
Executive Leadership				
R&D	Sales & Marketing	Technical Support	Human Resources	Customer Support
5 Paragraph Business Plan -------------- Operational Leadership	5 Paragraph Business Plan -------------- Operational Leadership	5 Paragraph Business Plan -------------- Operational Leadership	5 Paragraph Business Plan -------------- Operational Leadership	5 Paragraph Business Plan -------------- Operational Leadership
Key Leader Fragmentary Order	Key Leader Fragmentary Order	Key Leader Fragmentary Order	Key Leader Fragmentary Order	Key Leader Fragmentary Order
Debrief	Debrief	Debrief	Debrief	Debrief
After Action Review	After Action Review	After Action Review	After Action Review	After Action Review

Intelligence

Note how we have boiled all the way down to the individuals performing the actual daily work being conducted by the overall organization. Each individual fits within a FRAG-O that fits within an operational plan that fits within the overall "5 Paragraph Business Plan". An individual is introduced to the planning process and how the business functions when they are briefed the overall plan by 'executive leadership' and the operational plan by 'operational leadership' at the head of their specific business function. Their 'key leader' works off fragmentary orders, FRAG-Os, that are the same basic "5 Paragraph" format and pull elements from executive and operational plans. As key leaders excel, and are promoted to the operational leadership level, they build off the knowledge and experience gained by creating FRAG-Os to construct their own detailed operational "5 Paragraph Business Plan". Thorough understanding of the overall business functions leads to executive level comprehension and eventual promotion. The key is working off the same business planning template to conduct operations and improve the business over the long term.

Draw how intelligence flows in your organization:

"5 Paragraph Business Plan" - Pitch Deck

The executive summary you've created using the METT-TSL template is your starting point for creating a pitch deck. Start by creating 14 slides. First slide is your orientation. This is when you deliver your elevator pitch. The elevator pitch is a combination of the situation and mission paragraphs. Basically, it's the problem/opportunity statement followed by the mission statement and the 5 w's of your company. The elevator pitch entices audience members to pay attention.

Ex. "Entrepreneurs NEED a structured method for growing their business while maintaining control of the various business functions. The VALUE of the "5 Paragraph Business Plan" is in its simplicity. - Based on the United States military's planning concepts, that have been honed over the past 240 years, the "5 Paragraph Business Plan" is an action-oriented and situationally flexible approach to conducting business management between executive leadership and operational leadership. Prioritize your business strategies and empower your workforce with the "5 Paragraph Business Plan".

Ex. "Business leaders NEED a method for delegating authority while maintaining control of various business functions. The VALUE of the "5 Paragraph Business Plan" is in its simplicity. - Based on the United States military's planning concepts, that have been honed over the past 240 years, the "5 Paragraph Business Plan" is an action-oriented and situationally flexible approach to conducting business management between executive leadership and operational leadership. Empower your business leaders today with the "5 Paragraph Business Plan".

Discuss the SALUTE report from the situation paragraph in Slide 2. Be clear and concise in your delivery. This one slide outlines WHY you are creating the venture. This leads straight into your big value proposition; the solution your company is providing to fix the problem. The execution slides (4-9) are based on the FRAG-Os you've created within the general plan under the execution paragraph. These FRAG-Os have all the details needed to construct the execution slides. Each slide will be questioned. A FRAG-O is required to back up each execution slide. For slide 11, grab the highlights from each sub-paragraph of the financials. These are the golden nuggets, which entice potential investors or stakeholders. Slide 11 lines up the audience for the big ASK on slide 12. This is the climax of the pitch! - next, on slide 13, describe the leadership of the company, the management team and a brief summary of their roles. Conclude with a wrap up elevator pitch and post your contact information on the last slide; slide 14.

Make sure everyone you are pitching to gets a take-away of some kind.

- Business Cards.
- Promotional Material.
- White Paper.
- Product; Additional Marketing Materials.

Your pitch must entertain, educate & empower the audience to commit action.

SLIDE 1: Orientation [METT-TSL] - 'Elevator Pitch'.

        30 Seconds to Share the Scope of your Vision.

SLIDE 2: Situation [SALUTE] - Problem That You Solve.

SLIDE 3: Mission - Your Solution, Company Concept.

SLIDE 4: Execution - Product Offering.

        DEMONSTRATION.

SLIDE 5: Execution - Market Potential.

SLIDE 6: Execution - Competitive Landscape.

SLIDE 7: Execution - Competitive Strategy.

SLIDE 8: Execution - Economic Model.

SLIDE 9: Execution – Operations.

        Bring your passion.

SLIDE 10: Admin/Logistics – Financials.

SLIDE 11: Admin/Logistics - Funding, Progress Made Thus Far.

SLIDE 12: the ASK!

        DEFINE YOUR ASK.

SLIDE 13: Command / Signal - Management Team & Roles.

SLIDE 14: Command / Signal - Contact Information * Concluding 'Elevator Pitch'.

        LISTEN TO AUDIENCE FEEDBACK.

Be prepared to ask questions of your audience members and to receive feedback. Have a prepared list of open-ended questions for your audience to test their comprehension of your plan and the offering you provide. Only take advice from qualified sources.

LISTEN to the audience feedback and respond to questions. Write everything down. If the audience provides you with comments, concerns, suggestions or offerings write them down. Physically pull out a pen and paper and write them down; right there in front of everybody. Immediately write everything down. This is your debrief. The moments following your pitch are the absolute most valuable lessons learned. LISTEN to the audience. Empower them with takeaways and add VALUE.

Lastly, make sure everyone you are pitching to has a take-away. Prioritize who you give marketing material to such as event judges, investors, potential shareholders etc. Make a lasting impression that inspires someone to follow up with you and support your efforts. Take the time to share your biggest VALUE offering with everyone who attended the pitch. Be sure to provide a strong call to action to everyone who viewed your pitch. A few examples may be, "Share my product with a friend; purchase our product today; share our service offering with your network". This builds champions out of audience members.

After Action – Act, Debrief, Learn, Train, Act…

Gather the constructive criticism and lessons learned then apply them to your plan. The more you pitch, the better you get. Refine your plan. Stay the course. Success is based on your ability to create an attractive venture that you and others wish to participate in. Prove your desire, comprehension, and commitment to action.

Desire creates passion, which breeds motivation and confidence to pursue the unknown for the sake of adding value to a greater cause.

Comprehension through study and experience cultivates expertise, which develops into a clear understanding of the challenges ahead and how best to prepare a structure for organizing the chaos.

Action through a desire to fully comprehend the situation your venture faces; assess yourself, your team, your organization, and engage with peers to learn and understand through experience, which blossoms into wisdom that is used to target an opportunity for providing VALUE through the strengths of your organization.

Build your plan. Develop a clear and concise pitch. Illustrate to others the size and scope of the problem/opportunity at hand and the population in NEED. See if they'd like to learn more about the VALUE you are offering.

Use this guidebook, the following templates, and workbook to outline your thoughts and develop your own "5 Paragraph Business Plan". Visit 5Paragraph.com for more tips, tricks, and tutorials. Schedule a call with one of our advisors. We also provide in house seminars, workshops, and programming for organized retreats. Contact us right now at 5Paragraph.com

5 Paragraph Business Plan

TEMPLATE

Orientation – Executive Summary

- Problem- Opportunity Statement.
- Business Concept and Product or Service.
- Description of the Target Market.
- Technology and Operational Issues.
- The Team.
- Economics.
- Financial Highlights.
- Financial Need.

I. Situation

A. Industry; Market Research & Analysis
  Define the problem that your company will address.
  1. Industry's Composition, Disposition, Strength.
     - Summarize the industry in which the proposed business will operate.
       o Market segmentation and target market.
       o Estimated market share and sales figures.
     - SALUTE: Size Activity Location Uniform Time Equipment.
       o Buyer demographics and buyer behavior.
       o Definition of your relevant market and customer overview.
     - <u>S</u>ize of the market and the overall trends in <u>a</u>ctivity.
     - <u>L</u>ocation where business is conducted [online/brick & mortar].
     - <u>U</u>niform; Average consumer: age, gender, marital status, college level, household income.
     - <u>T</u>ime of typical purchase.
     - <u>E</u>quipment needed to sell - equipment need to purchase.
  2. Capabilities & Limitations
     - Discuss briefly industry size (in Dollars) and annual growth rate (%).
     - Discuss the structure of the industry at present.
     - Highlight key trends in the industry at present.
     - **highlight Key trends in the industry.**
     - Fluctuations in the market in the past 3-5 years.
       - Why this is good, bad or, ugly.
  3. Market's Most Likely Course of Action
     - Current trends [3-6 months].
     - Long term trends [2-5 years].
     - Provide standard financial ratios for the industry
  4. Market's Most Probable Course of Action

49

- Where the market is going based upon intelligence analysis.
- Ongoing market evaluation.
- Determine the key success factors for the industry and draw conclusions.

5. Market's Most Dangerous Course of Action; **Critical Risks, Problems & Assumptions**
   - **Discuss assumptions implicit in the plan.**
   - Identify and discuss any major problems and other risks.
   - Address assumptions/potential problems/risks critical to the success of the venture.

B. Friendly Forces

6. Higher command's mission & intent
   - List the large competitors that will be disrupted by your activity.
   - List the perceived objectives of key industry players.

7. Adjacent Companies; competition – friend or foe
   - **Competition and competitive edges.**
   - Location –
     o Collaborator's locations.
     o direct competitor's locations.
   - Goals & objectives.

8. Supporting companies
   - Supplier raw materials, goods, items etc.
   - Customer service, digital personal assistance, scheduling software, customer relationship management software etc.

C. Attachments/Detachments
   - **Supporting professional advisors and services.**
   - Freelance.
   - Interns.

D. Civil/Terrain Considerations
   - Work necessary for business.
     - Attend trade show, meetings, events, conventions.

II. **Mission;** Company, Concept, Goods/ Products/ Services
- The Company and Concept
- The Product and or Service
- Entry and Growth Strategy

  Who you are helping; basic customer profile [soccer moms, veterans, elderly]

  What you are doing to help; good, product, service

  Where customers purchase

  When is this happening - timeline

  Why are you doing this? - show us the passion

50

III. Execution

A. Commander's Intent; Leadership's Goal – Company's Directive
  1. Center of Gravity; biggest pot of gold in the market
     - Revenue drivers and profit margins (contribution margins).
  2. Critical Vulnerability; low hanging fruit
     - Fixed and variable costs.
     - Operating leverage and its implications.
     - **Startup costs.**
  3. Exploitation Plan;
     - Marketing Strategy – customer-centric
       o **Overall marketing strategy.**
       o **Pricing.**
     - Sales Strategy – experience based
       o **The selling cycles.**
       o Sales tactics.
       o **Distribution.**
     - Promotion Strategy
       o **Advertising and sale promotions.**
       o Publicity.
     - Customer Service/ Support
       o **Warranty or guarantee policies.**
  4. Desired End State
     - Breakeven chart and calculation.
     - **Profit durability.**
     - Satisfied customer.
     - Returning customer. > brand ambassador

B. Concept of the Operations
  5. Scheme of Maneuver
     - **Overall economic model.**
     - Marketing plan.
     - Walk through what it should look like when executing the plan.
     - All moving parts are assigned a task, conditions and, standards.
  6. Design & Development Plan
     - Development status and tasks.
     - Difficulties and risks.
     - Product improvement and new products.
     - Costs.
     - Proprietary issues.
       o Emergency roles – basic processes for handling crisis.
       o Lowest level leadership.

51

C. Tasks
- Delegation of authority – assumption of responsibility.
- Priority based on market variables [point of friction].
  - o Research and development, sales.

D. Coordinating Instructions; Operations Plan
- Operating model and cycle.
- Operations strategy.
- Geographic location.
- Facilities, equipment and, improvements.
- Capacity levels and inventory management.
- Legal issues affecting operations.
  - o Identify key leadership.
  - o Role of leadership.
    - Teams.
    - Role of team members.

IV. **Administration/Logistics**- The Economics of the Business

A. Administration –basic business functions
- Highlights of the financial statements
- Cost controls
- Documents to be developed for this section (put financial statements in appendix)
- Pro forma income statements
- Pro forma balance sheets
- Pro forma cash flow analysis

FINANCIAL PLAN
(create 5 years of pro forma statements; put them in the appendix)

PROPOSED COMPANY OFFERING

- Desired financing
- Offering (this is the deal structure-your pitch for money)
- Capitalization
- Use of funds
- Investor's return (exit strategy)

B. Logistics – the moving parts associated with routine business

- Human resources, customer care, hospitality
- Employment and other agreements, stock options and, bonus plans
- Include contingencies for emergency situations

V. **Command/ Signal**

A. Signal; communication to leadership and "go-to" processes for given scenarios

Primary

Alternate

Contingency

Emergency

B. Command; **management team**

Location of Key Leaders

Succession of Command

- Organization.
- Key management and personnel.
- Management compensation and ownership.
- Other current investors.
- Employment and other agreements, stock options and, bonus plans.
- Board of directors or board of advisors.
- Other shareholders, rights and, restrictions.

Resources

"The Operations Process" Army Publication; PUBLIC release, distribution unlimited
The Operations Process TRADOC. Retrieved 16 January 2013 ; FM 5-0, paragraph
1-130. Headquarters Department of The Army. March 2010. Web. January 2016

"Warfighting" Marine Corps Publication; PUBLIC release, distribution unlimited
MCDP 1 Warfighting U.S. Marine Corps, Pg. 88 Retrieved 16 January 2013
Department of The Navy; Headquarters Marine Corps. June 1997. January 2016

"ADRP 5-0 The Orders Process" Army Publication; PUBLIC release, distribution unlimited
FM 5-0, paragraph 1-19. Headquarters Department of The Army. May 2012.
January 2016

"The Nuts and Bolts of Great Business Plans" Syracuse: 2014. Print.
http://whitman.syr.edu/programs-and-academics/centers-and-
institutes/falcone/for-students/panasci/pdf/nutsandbolts.pdf Whitman School
of Management. November 2014. Web. January 2016

5

Tips, tricks, and tutorials found at
5Paragraph.com

Complete a call with one of our advisors
and receive a free workbook to get you
started.

We offer in-person advising and instruction
to include corporate retreats, event
workshops, and keynotes by U.S. military
veterans who are adding
VALUE to the world.

Glossary of Terms

Adjacent unit - organizations with a similar size and mission; may include different elements of an overall organization such as teams, divisions, regions etc.; in a broader market, an adjacent unit may be considered competitors or direct competitors that are friendly and wish to collaborate.

Accrual - the action or process of accruing something; cash-flow and accrual are different with accrual being money gained by the accrual of interest.

Assumptions - to lay claim; to pretend to have or be; made up figures based on factual information.

Capital - money and property a business owns outright.

Capital acquisitions - assets acquired through the use of capital.

Capitalization - provision of capital for a company, or the conversion of income or assets into capital.

Cash flow analysis - examination of a company's inflows & outflows of cash during a specific period.

Cash flow sensitivity - effect of financial constraints as captured by the firm's propensity to save cash out of cash flows.

Center of gravity - largest target market in your industry given the solution you currently offer or will offer in the future, the biggest pot of gold you aim to capitalize on -- (See also critical vulnerability).

Contribution margin - selling price minus variable cost, measures the ability of a company to cover variable costs with revenue.

Contribution margin ratio - the percentage of revenue that remains once variable costs and expenses have been covered.

Cost of goods sold - cost of materials and direct labor needed to produce the goods; excludes distribution costs and cost of sales; deduct cost of goods sold from revenue to project contribution margin.

Critical vulnerability - area within the market's center of gravity the is most vulnerable to attack, also known as the market entry point, the critical vulnerability provides a scope of objectives that must be compiled to create your exploitation plan.

Debt to equity ratio - used to measure a company's financial leverage, calculated by dividing a company's total liabilities by its stockholders' equity. The D/E ratio indicates how much debt a company is using to finance its assets relative to the amount of value represented in shareholders' equity.

Disbursements - the payment of money from a fund.

Emotional intelligence - an individual's capacity to be aware of their own emotions providing them the ability to potentially control and express their emotions, some are more capable of handling interpersonal relationships with a greater sense of empathy and overall spiritual understanding.

Exploitation plan - plan for attacking the critical vulnerability within a greater market's center of gravity; the exploitation plan is a "30,000 foot" perspective on how to attack a given market.

Equity - percentage of ownership in a company; the value of the shares issued by a company.

Financial ratios - determining financial relationships between statements to understand the logic associated with the financial viability of a business; return on investment, return on assets.

Fixed cost - business costs that are constant, such as rent; independent of any business activity.

Gross margin - total sales revenue minus cost of goods sold.

Investor's return - the benefit to an investor for putting capital into a business.

Key metrics - any data or metrics used to capture the performance of a business.

Market segmentation - the process of dividing an entire market into multiple customer segments.

Margin - the percentage of profit in the sales price; sales minus cost of goods sold.

Operating leverage - measurement of a combination of fixed and variable costs. A business with high sales and a very high gross margin and fewer fixed costs and variable costs has a higher operating leverage.

Profit - a financial gain; the difference between the amount earned and the amount spent, calculated by taking revenue minus cost of goods sold minus cost of sale and additional fixed costs to revenue gained.

Profit durability - the potential to gain a profit and sustain profits for a given period.

Pro forma - done or produced as a matter of form or politeness.

Proprietary issues - disputes over ownership; regarding patents, trademarks, copyrights etc.

Receipts - a written acknowledgement of items received through transaction.

Receivable collection period - the amount of time it takes to receive payment before an account is deemed to be outstanding or past due.

Revenue - income gained through business activity.

Securities - a financial instrument that represents ownership in a company.

Shareholder - an owner of shares in a company; part owner of the larger company. Determine equity by taking the amount of shares a shareholder possess, divided by the total amount of shares available in the company.

Target market - the particular group of consumers a business is focused on.

Variable cost - a cost which varies based on the level of output; directly associated with business activity; includes all costs associated with producing, selling and, distribution; raw materials, labor, sales force, energy consumption etc.

Additional terms	Definition

The 5 Paragraph Business Plan Workbook

Orientation – Executive Summary; METT-TSL

Mission:

Enemy (Problem-Opportunity):

Size   -

Activity   -

Location   -

Uniform   -

Time   -

Equipment   -

Team & Support:

Higher   -

Adjacent   -

Supporting   -

Terrain & Weather:

Space:

Logistics:

I. Situation

A. Industry; Market Research & Analysis
   Define the problem that your company will address.

   1. Industry's Composition, Disposition, Strength

      - Summarize the industry in which the proposed business will operate.
        o Market segmentation and target market.
        o Estimated market share and sales figures.

      - SALUTE: Size Activity Location Uniform Time Equipment
        o Buyer demographics and buyer behavior.
        o Definition of your relevant market and customer overview.

        - Size of the industry, scope of the target market.

        - Activity in the market and overall trend.

        - Location where business is conducted [online/brick & mortar].

        - Uniform; Average consumer: age, gender, marital status, college

          level, household income.

        - Time of typical purchase.

        - Equipment needed to sell - equipment need to purchase.

I. Situation

A. Industry; Market Research & Analysis

1. Industry's Composition, Disposition, Strength

Summary:

SALUTE:

      Size

      Activity

      Location

      Unit / uniform

      Time

      Equipment

2. Capabilities & Limitations
   - Highlight your overall capabilities for addressing the need within your target market.
   - Discuss the limitations your company has in providing it's offering to your target market.
     - Highlight how you have worked to create an efficient method for delivery, i.e. streamline your processes, develop a better product, offer a higher quality service etc.
   - Discuss potential negative effects that your company may encounter operating in your target industry.
     - Highlight how you have worked to mitigate those effects on your business.
   - Discuss briefly industry size (in Dollars) and annual growth rate (%).
   - Discuss the structure of the industry at present.
   - Highlight key trends in the industry at present.
   - **highlight Key trends in the industry.**
   - Fluctuations in the market in the past 3-5 years.
     - Why this is good, bad or, ugly.
3. Market's Most Likely Course of Action
   - Current trends [3-6 months].
   - Long term trends [2-5 years].
   - Provide standard financial ratios for the industry.
4. Market's Most Probable Course of Action
   - Where the market is going based upon intelligence analysis.
   - Ongoing market evaluation.
   - Determine the key success factors for the industry and draw conclusions.
5. Market's Most Dangerous Course of Action; **Critical Risks, Problems & Assumptions**
   - **Discuss assumptions implicit in the plan.**
   - Identify and discuss any major problems and other risks.
   - Address assumptions/potential problems/risks critical to the success of the venture.

2. Capabilities & Limitations

3. Market's Most Likely Course of Action

4. Market's Most Probable Course of Action

5. Market's Most Dangerous Course of Action;
   Critical Risks, Problems and Assumptions

B. Friendly Forces

    1. Higher Command's Mission & Intent
- List the large competitors that will be disrupted by your activity.
- List the perceived objectives of key industry players.

    2. Adjacent Companies; competition – friend or foe
- Competition and competitive edges.

- Location –
  o Collaborator's locations.
  o Direct competitor's locations.

- Goals & Objectives

    3. Supporting Companies
- Supplier raw materials, goods, items etc.
- Customer service, digital personal assistance, scheduling software, customer relationship management software etc.

C. Attachments/ Detachment
- **Supporting professional advisors and services.**
- Freelance.
- Interns.

D. Civil/ Terrain Considerations
- Work necessary for business.
  o Attend trade show, meetings, events, conventions.

B. Friendly Forces

6. Higher Command's Mission & Intent

7. Adjacent Companies; competition – friend or foe

Location –

Goals & Objectives -

8. Supporting Companies

Location –

Goals & Objectives -

C. Attachments/ Detachment

Location –

Goals & Objectives -

D. Civil/ Terrain Considerations

II. Mission; company, concept, goods/ products/ services

Mission directive; what you are doing about the problem/ opportunity.

There are distinct objectives for every mission. The same is true for business. There are distinct objectives that must be accomplished in order for the mission to be a success. This overarching mission will be the foundation for all other business operations and should include the values and ethics of the overall organization. It is key to constructing a long-term business strategy.

- The Company and Concept
- The Product and or Service
- Entry and Growth Strategy

Who you are helping; basic customer profile [soccer moms, veterans, elderly]

What you are doing to help; good, product, service

Where customers purchase

When is this happening - timeline

Why you are doing this - show us the passion

III. **Execution**

    A. Commander's Intent; leadership's goal – company's directive
        1. Center of Gravity; biggest pot of gold in the market
- Revenue drivers and profit margins (contribution margins).

        2. Critical Vulnerability; low hanging fruit
- Fixed and variable costs.
- Operating leverage and its implications.
- **Startup costs.**

II. Mission; company, concept, goods/products/services

Company -

Concept -

Why -

III. **Execution**

A. Commander's Intent; leadership's goal – company's directive

4. Center of Gravity; biggest pot of gold in the market

Critical Vulnerability; low hanging fruit

B. Concept of the Operations

1. Scheme of Maneuver
   - **Overall economic model**.
   - Marketing plan.
   - Walk through what it should look like when executing the plan.
   - All moving parts are assigned a task, conditions and, standards.

2. Design & Development Plan
   - Development status and tasks.
   - Difficulties and risks.
   - Product improvement and new products.
   - Costs.
   - Proprietary issues.
   - Emergency roles – basic processes for handling crisis.
   - Lowest level leadership.

C. Tasks
   - Delegation of authority – assumption of responsibility.
   - Priority based on market variables [point of friction].
     o Research and development, sales, marketing.

D. Coordinating Instructions; operations plan
   - Operating model and cycle.
   - Operations strategy.
   - Geographic location.
   - Facilities, equipment and, improvements.
   - Capacity levels and inventory management & control.
   - Legal issues affecting operations.
     o Identify key leadership.
     o Role of leadership.
       - Teams.
       - Role of team members.
         o Gear specific to team member.
         o Equipment specific to mission.
         o Additional specific consideration.

B. Concept of the Operations

1. Scheme of Maneuver

2. Design & Development Plan

C. Tasks

D. Coordinating Instructions; Operations Plan

IV. **Administration/ Logistics** the Economics of the Business

    A. Administration –basic business functions.
- Highlights of the financial statements.
- Cost controls.
- Documents to be developed for this section (put financial statements in appendix).
- Pro forma income statements.
- Pro forma balance sheets.
- Pro forma cash flow analysis.

FINANCIAL PLAN **(create 5 years of pro forma statements; put them in the appendix)**

PROPOSED COMPANY OFFERING
- Desired financing.
- Offering (this is the deal structure-your pitch for money).
- Capitalization.
- Use of funds.
- Investor's return (exit strategy).

B. Logistics – the moving parts associated with routine business
- Human resources, customer care, hospitality.
- Employment and other agreements, stock options and, bonus plans.
- Include contingencies for emergency situations.

IV. **Administration/ Logistics** the Economics of the Business

    A. Administration –basic business functions

FINANCIAL PLANS **(create 5 years of pro forma statements; put them in the appendix)**

PROPOSED COMPANY OFFERING

B. Logistics – the moving parts associated with routine business

V. Command/ Signal

A. Signal; communication to leadership and "go-to" processes for given scenarios

Primary method of communication on a routine basis.

Alternate method of communication for immediate action.

Contingency plan method of communication.

Emergency communication plan to call immediate action to the entire organization.

B. Command; **management team**

Leadership biographies.

Mission specific expertise.

Leadership resumes.

Location of Key Leaders

Office address.

Mailing address.

Area of responsibility.

Succession of Command
- Organization.
- Key management and personnel.
- Management compensation and ownership.
- Other current investors.
- Employment and other agreements, stock options and, bonus plans.
- Board of directors or board of advisors.
- Other shareholders, rights and, restrictions.

V. **Command/ Signal**

A. Signal; communication to leadership and "go-to" processes for given scenarios.

Primary   -

Alternate   -

Contingency   -

Emergency   -

B. Command; **management team**

Location of Key Leaders

Succession of Command

Appendices:

Item	Title

5

Tips, tricks, and tutorials found at
5Paragraph.com

Complete a call with one of our advisors
and receive a free workbook to get you
started.

We offer in-person advising and instruction
to include corporate retreats, event
workshops, and keynotes by U.S. military
veterans who are adding
VALUE to the world.

Need advice on how best to implement the

"5 Paragraph Business Plan"

Our advisors work with scaling businesses

to create an outline for the entire

organization to work with,

keeping everyone on the same page

Schedule a FREE advisory call today at

5Paragraph.com

* 9 7 8 0 6 9 2 8 8 5 8 9 5 *